Author: Cath Senker is a writer of non-fiction for children on diverse subjects such as history, world religions, and the environment. In 2018, she won the Educational Writers' Award.

Author acknowledgements:

A team of children have helped with this writing adventure. The author would like to thank them for their contribution:

Nour Alsaleh (age 14) pages 31, 70; Matthew Dunkerley (age 10) pages 6, 38, 70; Alexander Hawkins (age 11) pages 48, 77, 95, 97; Shira Rosenberg (age 11) pages 20, 31, 32 (tip), 59, 65, 70.

The author would like to acknowledge these sources:

Pages 31–2: Movie-maker from Helen Stockton, *Teaching creative writing: ideas, exercises, resources and lesson plans for teachers of creative-writing classes,* Constable and Robinson Ltd, 2013, p. 64
Page 65: Quotation from *JK Rowling: Behind the Magic* by Cath Senker, Random House, 2021
Page 74: Journey stick from RSPB Wild writing https://www.rspb.org.uk/fun-and-learning/for-teachers/schools-wild-challenge/activities/wild-writing/
Page 76: How to write a detective story: 7 keys to a killer whodunnit https://www.nownovel.com/blog/write-detective-story-7-keys/
Page 96: Writing competitions https://www.christopherfielden.com/short-story-tips-and-writing-advice/

Photo credits: pg. 31
sondem, Kostya Zatulin, NikoNomad, Teo Tarras / Shutterstock.com

This edition published in Great Britain in MMXXII
by Scribblers, an imprint of
The Salariya Book Company Ltd
25 Marlborough Place,
Brighton BN1 1UB
www.salariya.com

Text © Cath Senker MMXXII
Illustrations © Isobel Lundie MMXXII
English language © The Salariya Book Company Ltd MMXXII

All rights reserved. No part of this publication may be reproduced, stored in or introduced into a retrieval system or transmitted in any form, or by any means (electronic, mechanical, photocopying, recording or otherwise) without the written permission of the publisher. Any person who does any unauthorised act in relation to this publication may be liable to criminal prosecution and civil claims for damages.

ISBN: 978-1-913971-37-3

1 3 5 7 9 8 6 4 2

A CIP catalogue record for this book is available from the British Library.

Printed in China.

Printed on paper from sustainable sources.

This book is sold subject to the conditions that it shall not, by way of trade or otherwise, be lent, resold, hired out, or otherwise circulated without the publisher's prior consent in any form or binding or cover other than that in which it is published and without similar condition being imposed on the subsequent purchaser.

Visit
www.salariya.com
for our online catalogue and
free fun stuff.

Illustrator: Isobel Lundie is an illustrator and designer who works in Brighton. Since graduating from Kingston University with a First-Class Honours in illustration and animation, she has specialised in children's publishing. Isobel has been lucky enough to make books for Salariya, Usborne, Random House, DK and the Good Book Company. She uses a wide variety of materials such as collage papers, pencil, ink and digital media. She likes creating detailed work with wacky characters that makes children laugh.

WHAT SHALL WE WRITE?

Written by
Cath Senker

Illustrated by
Isobel Lundie

This book belongs to:

CONTENTS PAGE

Chapter 1: Inspiration

10 Read, read, read
12 Feed your imagination
16 Gather your thoughts

Chapter 2: Planning

20 Time and space
22 Creating characters
24 Life stories
26 Heroes and villains
28 Whose story?
31 Story settings
34 Plot

This book is packed with useful tips!

HELP!

Chapter 3: Writing

38 Once upon a time...
40 Description
42 Showing and telling
44 Spice it up
46 Dialogue
48 Pace
52 Happily ever after?

Chapter 4: Genres

- 56 Fairy-tale mash-up
- 58 Comic strip
- 62 Animation
- 65 Real-life stories
- 68 Science fiction
- 70 Fantasy
- 72 Wildlife adventure
- 76 Whodunnit
- 80 Creepy story
- 82 Flash fiction
- 84 Poetry

Lots of spaces for you to write into

Chapter 5: Presenting your work

- 88 Try and try again
- 92 Mind your language
- 94 Feedback
- 96 Sharing your work
- 100 Write to a publisher

102 Glossary

104 Index

INTRODUCTION

A sudden hush envelops the hall as the announcer walks briskly to the microphone. She clears her throat and raises her eyes to a sea of faces gathered for the first Young Writers Award Ceremony. Heart racing, sweaty palms, rapid breathing — you can't wait to find out. Will your treasured story win a prize?

This could be you. Or perhaps you're proudly reading your latest story to your auntie, your dog... or silently to yourself.

Whatever your creative writing ambitions, this book is for you. It will let you run free with your ideas and help you organise them to create a story.

HELP!

Whatever you want to write, you'll need some basic skills to help you on the way:

- Finding inspiration
- Planning
- Developing a plot
- Creating a setting
- Crafting characters
- Writing a good opening and ending
- Improving your writing

How to use this book

The first part is all about finding inspiration. Once you've decided on your idea, go to the planning section. Refer also to the genre section for the kind of story you want to create. Now it's time to start writing, following the tips from the writing chapter.

When you've drafted your story, work through the editing chapter to improve and check it. Then it's ready for your audience — whether it's a national competition, your auntie or your dog.

Use this checklist to make the most out of this book and write your best story ever!

- [ ] Finding inspiration
- [ ] Planning my story
- [ ] Deciding on the genre
- [ ] Drafting
- [ ] Editing
- [ ] Sharing my story

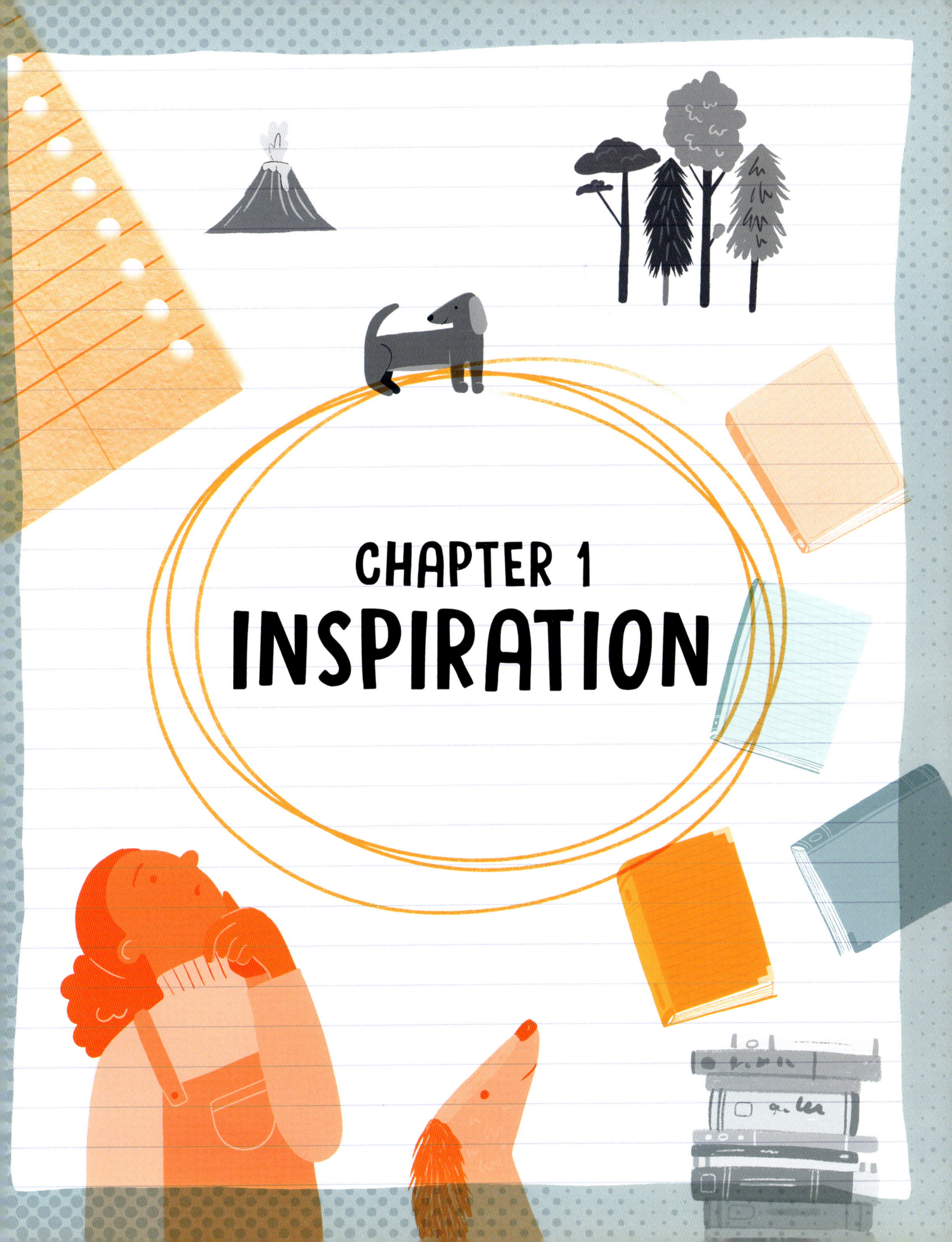

CHAPTER 1
INSPIRATION

READ, READ, READ!

To write well, it is vital to be a keen reader. As you read, you meet new words, see how sentences are made and work out how stories are put together. You learn without even thinking about it.

What kind of story do you enjoy?

Maybe you enjoy escaping to other worlds in fantasy or science-fiction books, such as *Artemis Fowl* or the *School for Good and Evil* series. Or perhaps you prefer tales based on real life, such as Onjali Q. Raúf's *The Boy at the Back of the Class*.

Do you like being shocked and scared reading creepy stories, whodunnits or tales of adventures? Or do you love to laugh with a funny story? Perhaps poetry is your thing — poems can say a lot in just a few words.

If you're into drawing, you might prefer comic books or animations.

Activity: Identify the features of a story

See if you can find all of these features in one of your favourite books. Note what you like about them.

- Plot — what happens in the story
- Setting — where the story happens
- Characters — people (or animals or objects)
- Dialogue — characters talking to each other
- Descriptions — parts that explain the scene or action

Name:

Plot:

Setting:

Characters:

Dialogue:

Descriptions:

Name:

Plot:

Setting:

Characters:

Dialogue:

Descriptions:

Name:

Plot:

Setting:

Characters:

Dialogue:

Descriptions:

Name:

Plot:

Setting:

Characters:

Dialogue:

Descriptions:

FEED YOUR IMAGINATION

Your most important tool is your imagination. Feed it by reading books, watching films or researching online. Here are some other ways to get inspired.

Real life
- Friends, family and people you know
- Celebrities — musicians, artists, authors
- Sport: stories about winners and losers
- Animals

Events
- In the past, the present or imagining the future
- In your local area, your country or the world
- Disasters — anything from a cracked cup to the Covid-19 pandemic

Objects
- Around the house
- From nature
- In a museum

Places
- Home or away
- Natural world
- Space

Activity: Idea cloud

1. Draw a large cloud. Write or draw an idea for a topic or character in the middle. It might be a magical creature, an animal, a household object or an event in history.
2. Write words linked to it or draw them if you prefer.
3. Think of an idea for a story. Ask questions. What if something happens? How? When? Then what?
4. If you don't like your first idea cloud, try again.

Here's my idea cloud:

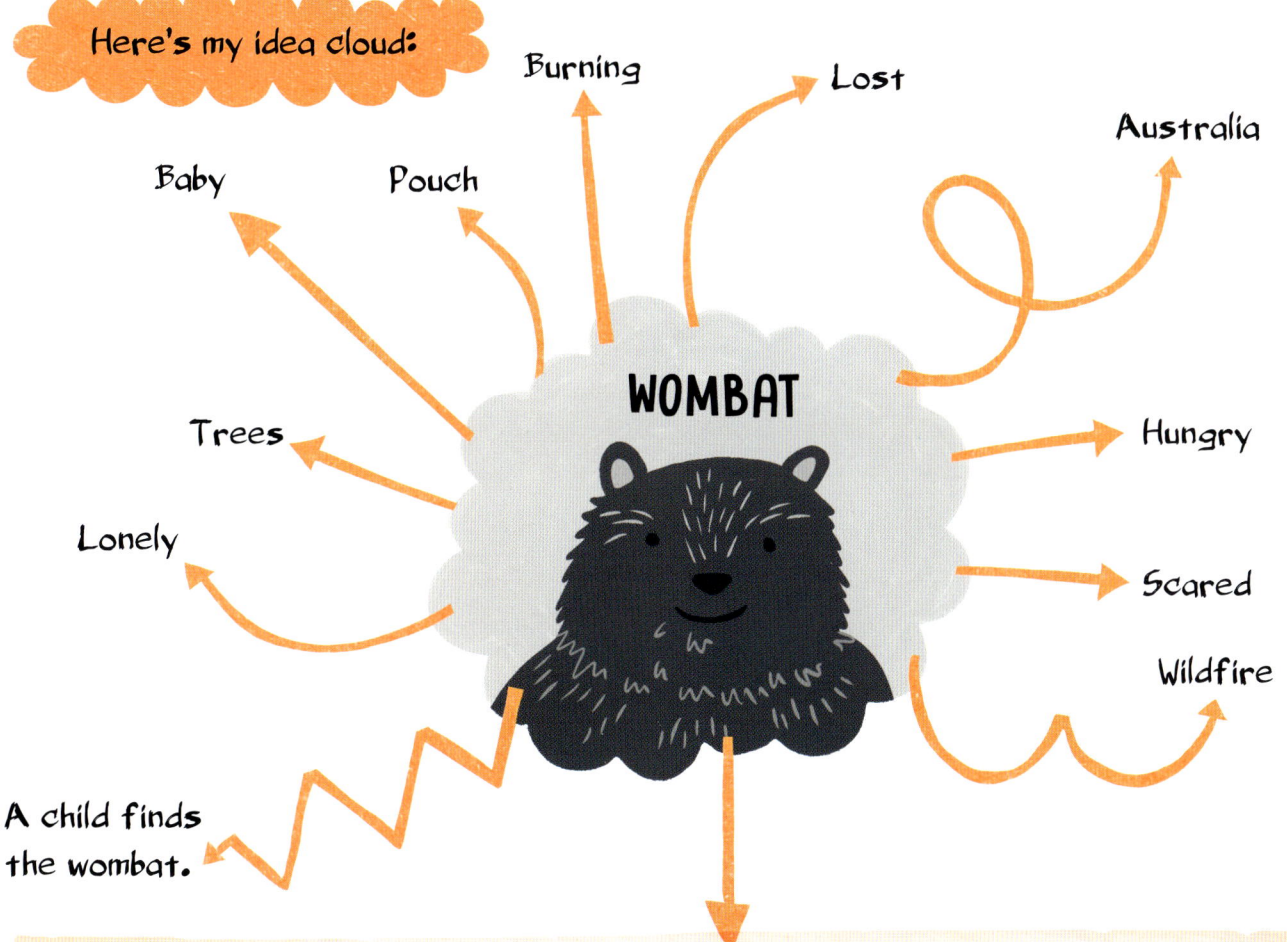

Burning, Lost, Australia, Baby, Pouch, WOMBAT, Hungry, Trees, Scared, Lonely, Wildfire, A child finds the wombat.

This could be a story about a baby wombat rescued in a terrifying wildfire in the Australian outback.
What if something happens? A child finds the wombat.
How? When? Then what?

Idea cloud

WHAT SHALL WE WRITE?

Written by
Cath Senker

Illustrated by
Isobel Lundie

This book belongs to:

CONTENTS PAGE

Chapter 1: Inspiration

- 10   Read, read, read
- 12   Feed your imagination
- 16   Gather your thoughts

Chapter 2: Planning

This book is packed with useful tips!

- 20   Time and space
- 22   Creating characters
- 24   Life stories
- 26   Heroes and villains
- 28   Whose story?
- 31   Story settings
- 34   Plot

HELP!

Chapter 3: Writing

- 38   Once upon a time...
- 40   Description
- 42   Showing and telling
- 44   Spice it up
- 46   Dialogue
- 48   Pace
- 52   Happily ever after?

Chapter 4: Genres

Lots of spaces for you to write into

- 56 Fairy-tale mash-up
- 58 Comic strip
- 62 Animation
- 65 Real-life stories
- 68 Science fiction
- 70 Fantasy
- 72 Wildlife adventure
- 76 Whodunnit
- 80 Creepy story
- 82 Flash fiction
- 84 Poetry

Chapter 5: Presenting your work

- 88 Try and try again
- 92 Mind your language
- 94 Feedback
- 96 Sharing your work
- 100 Write to a publisher

102 Glossary

104 Index

INTRODUCTION

A sudden hush envelops the hall as the announcer walks briskly to the microphone. She clears her throat and raises her eyes to a sea of faces gathered for the first Young Writers Award Ceremony. Heart racing, sweaty palms, rapid breathing — you can't wait to find out. Will your treasured story win a prize?

This could be you. Or perhaps you're proudly reading your latest story to your auntie, your dog... or silently to yourself.

Whatever your creative writing ambitions, this book is for you. It will let you run free with your ideas and help you organise them to create a story.

HELP!

Whatever you want to write, you'll need some basic skills to help you on the way:

- Finding inspiration
- Planning
- Developing a plot
- Creating a setting
- Crafting characters
- Writing a good opening and ending
- Improving your writing

How to use this book

The first part is all about finding inspiration. Once you've decided on your idea, go to the planning section. Refer also to the genre section for the kind of story you want to create. Now it's time to start writing, following the tips from the writing chapter.

When you've drafted your story, work through the editing chapter to improve and check it. Then it's ready for your audience — whether it's a national competition, your auntie or your dog.

Use this checklist to make the most out of this book and write your best story ever!

- [ ] Finding inspiration
- [ ] Planning my story
- [ ] Deciding on the genre
- [ ] Drafting
- [ ] Editing
- [ ] Sharing my story

READ, READ, READ!

To write well, it is vital to be a keen reader. As you read, you meet new words, see how sentences are made and work out how stories are put together. You learn without even thinking about it.

What kind of story do you enjoy?

Maybe you enjoy escaping to other worlds in fantasy or science-fiction books, such as *Artemis Fowl* or the *School for Good and Evil* series. Or perhaps you prefer tales based on real life, such as Onjali Q. Raúf's *The Boy at the Back of the Class*.

Do you like being shocked and scared reading creepy stories, whodunnits or tales of adventures? Or do you love to laugh with a funny story? Perhaps poetry is your thing — poems can say a lot in just a few words.

If you're into drawing, you might prefer comic books or animations.

Activity: Identify the features of a story

See if you can find all of these features in one of your favourite books. Note what you like about them.

- Plot — what happens in the story
- Setting — where the story happens
- Characters — people (or animals or objects)
- Dialogue — characters talking to each other
- Descriptions — parts that explain the scene or action

Name:

Plot:

Setting:

Characters:

Dialogue:

Descriptions:

Name:

Plot:

Setting:

Characters:

Dialogue:

Descriptions:

Name:

Plot:

Setting:

Characters:

Dialogue:

Descriptions:

Name:

Plot:

Setting:

Characters:

Dialogue:

Descriptions:

FEED YOUR IMAGINATION

Your most important tool is your imagination. Feed it by reading books, watching films or researching online. Here are some other ways to get inspired.

Real life

- Friends, family and people you know
- Celebrities — musicians, artists, authors
- Sport: stories about winners and losers
- Animals

Events

- In the past, the present or imagining the future
- In your local area, your country or the world
- Disasters — anything from a cracked cup to the Covid-19 pandemic

Objects

- Around the house
- From nature
- In a museum

Places

- Home or away
- Natural world
- Space

Activity: Idea cloud

1. Draw a large cloud. Write or draw an idea for a topic or character in the middle. It might be a magical creature, an animal, a household object or an event in history.
2. Write words linked to it or draw them if you prefer.
3. Think of an idea for a story. Ask questions.
   What if something happens? How? When? Then what?
4. If you don't like your first idea cloud, try again.

Here's my idea cloud:

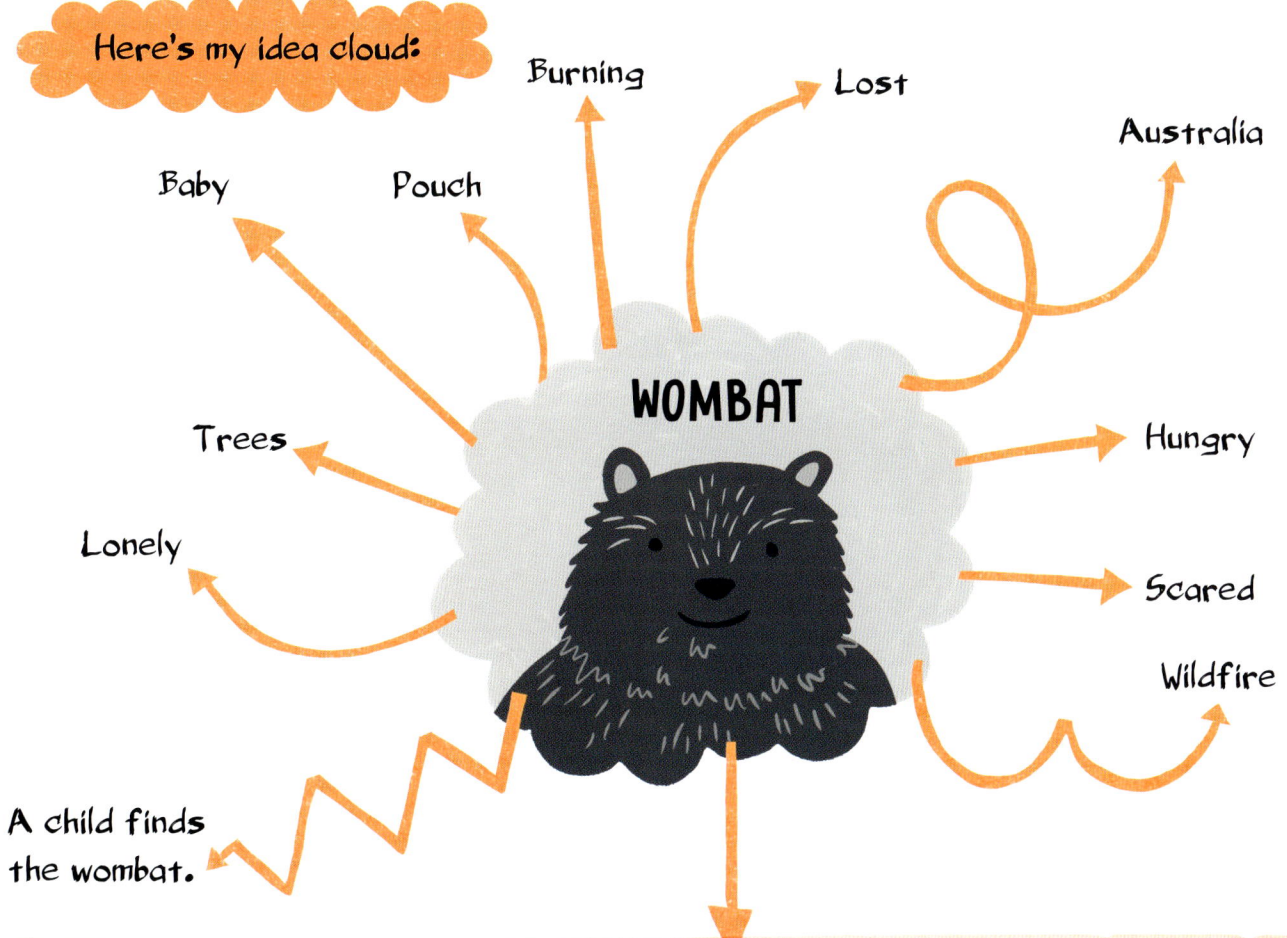

- Burning
- Lost
- Australia
- Baby
- Pouch
- WOMBAT
- Hungry
- Trees
- Scared
- Lonely
- Wildfire
- A child finds the wombat.

This could be a story about a baby wombat rescued in a terrifying wildfire in the Australian outback.
What if something happens? A child finds the wombat.
How? When? Then what?

Idea cloud

GATHER YOUR THOUGHTS

Ideas often come to you when your mind is relaxed. Thoughts will arrive while you're walking, playing, enjoying sports or quietly relaxing. Always have a notebook close by to write them down. Sometimes, ideas appear to me in the night. I make a note as soon as I wake up.

A striking snippet of conversation can inspire a story. I heard this one recently: 'When I was in Kenya, I learnt how to paraglide.'

Inspiration from objects

Collecting things can help you develop your ideas. Gather intriguing objects: an old map, a fridge magnet, a button. Ask before you borrow them! Check magazines for fascinating photos. Ask an adult to help you look online for photos of people, places, plants, animals or events.

Inspiration from nature

Outdoors in nature, look out for unusual pebbles, shells or pieces of wood.

Now think about how to use your photos and objects:
- Setting – pictures of places
- Characters – people or animals
- Plot – How might the people, animals, objects or events come into the story?

Activity: Note your ideas
Try these methods and see which works best for you.

List your ideas with bullet points

E.g.
- Setting – Australian outback
- Characters – wombat, child, wildlife volunteer
- Plot – baby wombat loses mother during wildfire and is rescued. What happens?

Your turn

- Setting

- Characters

- Plot

Mind map

- Rescue centre
- wildlife volunteer
- Child
- Australian outback
- Characters → Wombat
- Setting
- Lost wombat
- Child – wants to protect wildlife
- Wildfire
- Plot
- Wombat loses mother; cared for; returns to forest
- Solving environmental problems

Draw your mind map

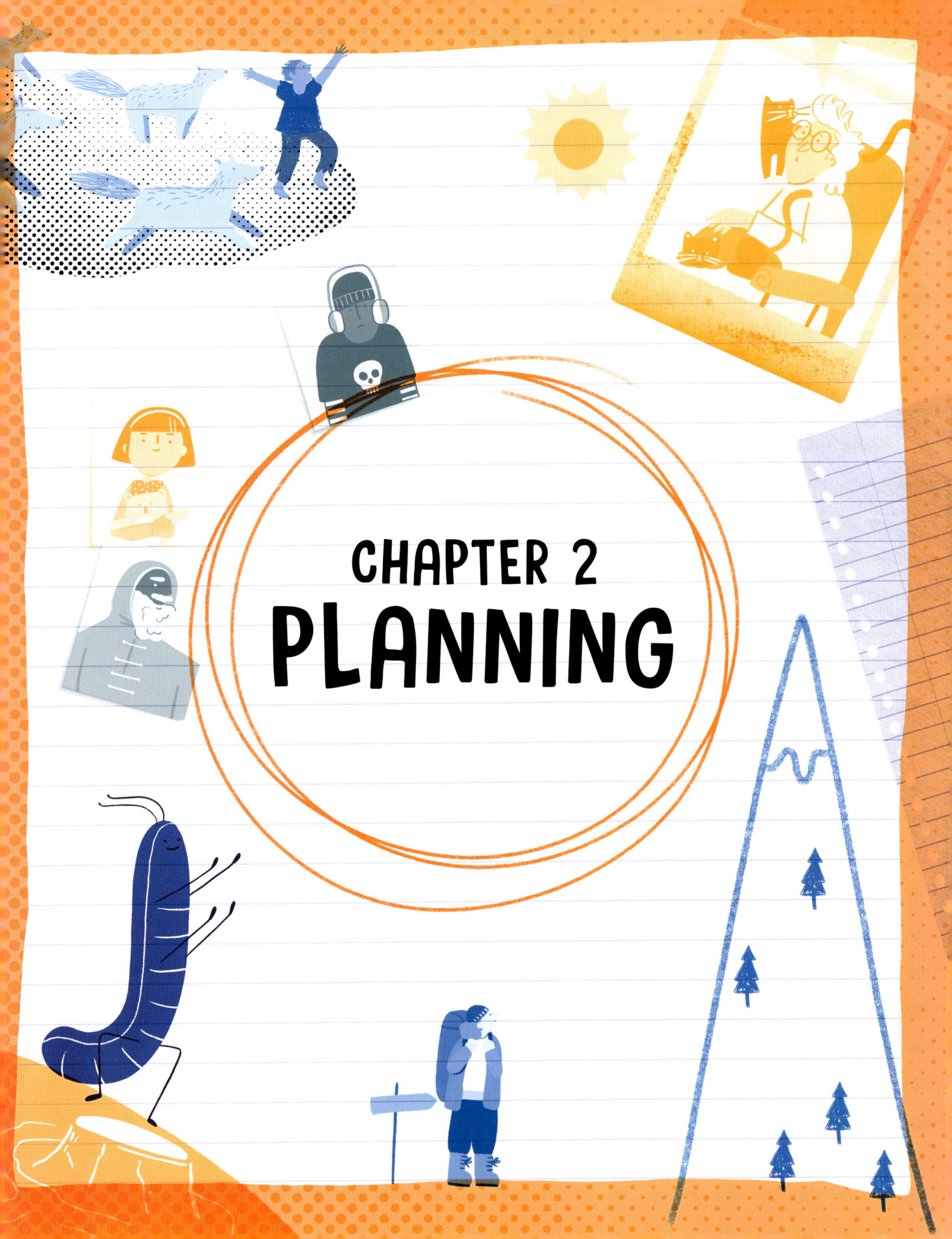

TIME AND SPACE

Whether you're writing for 10 minutes or 2 hours, make time and space for your writing.

TIP Get into the habit of writing for a few minutes every day.

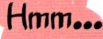
Hmm...

Where?

You might choose a special quiet space for writing. Perhaps you like to feel cosy, on the sofa with lots of cushions and a pet to cuddle up to. Maybe having books on the shelves around you will bring inspiration.

Maybe you prefer working while someone else is around. You can discuss your ideas with them.

When?

Writers usually like to have a routine. Think about what works for you.

Do you like to write for short chunks of time or longer ones?

Are you an early bird or night owl? I wrote an entire book by getting up early every day and writing for an hour or so.

'I have written about all **sorts** of topics; the weird and the wonderful. The harsh and the pleasant. For life is like that don't you think?' A. M. Dassu, author of *Boy, Everywhere*

Activity: Just write

Freewriting helps you to get into a writing routine. It is a great exercise for getting your ideas down — and it takes less than 5 minutes.

- Set a timer for 3 minutes.
- Start writing ideas for your story — the plot, setting or characters.
- Don't take your pencil off the page, and don't worry about spelling. It's important to sit and scribble non-stop.
- If you can't think what to write, just write 'blah blah' until a new thought arrives.
- Read what you wrote. Highlight any interesting ideas for your story.

Write here!

CREATING CHARACTERS

When you're inventing characters, start with what you know — yourself and the people around you. There are two parts to character:
- What does your character look like?
- What are they like?

TIP
Be imaginative and avoid stereotypes. It's true — most teachers at primary schools are women. But there are male teachers, too. Lots of girls play football, and some boys detest football.

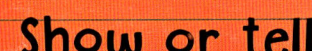

Show or tell

You can describe someone by telling your reader what they look like and how they behave:

Lenny has curly red hair. He is a cheerful boy who smiles a lot.

Instead of telling your reader, you can show them:

Lenny shook his head of bouncy red hair and smiled as wide as a slice of watermelon.

I've used a simile — saying his smile is like a slice of watermelon. This gives your reader a picture in their mind of Lenny.

'I'm always thinking about the stories I write — the characters and their plots go round in my head all day.' Robin Stevens

Activity: Describe yourself

Draw yourself or examine a photo. Write a list of six things about yourself, including what you look like and how you behave.

Me

Example:

1. Long dark hair
2. Glasses
3. Brown skin
4. Funny
5. Lively
6. Adventurous

What are the most striking things?

You can invent a new character using some remarkable features on your list.

'I'm sure I can easily climb that tree!' laughed Sam. (He's lively and adventurous.)

Your turn

- ....
- ....
- ....
- ....
- ....
- ....

....
....

What would you say?

Draw yourself here.

LIFE STORIES

Authors write life stories for their characters, describing their life in the past and present. Author Malorie Blackman creates a biography of three to four pages for each main character. It helps her characters to become like real people. You won't use all the information in your story. But knowing your characters as well as your closest friends helps you to work out what they would do in different situations.

It's best not to have too many characters. Each one has to play an important role in your story.

Activity: Write a life story

Answer these questions about your main character.

1. What is their name and where are they from?

2. Where did they live when they were little?

3. Where do they live now, and who with?

4. Who do they get on well with?

5. Who do they get on badly with?

6. What do they like?

7. What do they hate?

8. What do they want?

Hmm... Now I understand their actions!

Now imagine what your character would do in these different situations.

- They see a child being bullied.

- They find an injured animal.

- They see someone commit a crime.

- They find a large sum of money.

Do the same exercise for your other characters.

HEROES & VILLAINS

Stories are exciting when there is a conflict between goodies and baddies. Keep your reader on the edge of their seat, wondering who will triumph — and how.

Remember:

People aren't all good or all bad. They change through their lives because of their experiences and their relationships with others. They learn as they go along — both good and bad things.

Heroes sometimes hurt people, and villains might have a caring side. Create characters that are like real people so that your story is not predictable. If your reader can't guess what is going to happen next, it's more exciting.

HERO

What makes a hero?

Goodies don't have to be superheroes with special powers who rescue entire cities. Your tale might feature ordinary heroes — children who stand up to bullies, save a life or protect animals.

POW!

VILLAIN

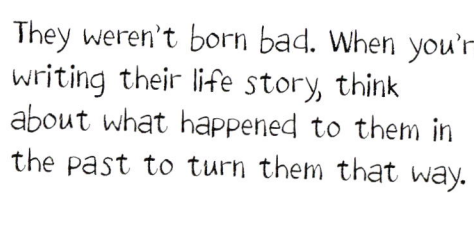

What makes a baddie?

They weren't born bad. When you're writing their life story, think about what happened to them in the past to turn them that way.

Activity: Examine a villain and a hero

Choose a villain and a hero from a favourite book or film.
Answer these questions:
- What are they like when they are young?
- What happens to them?
- How do their experiences change them?
- How does their past make them the way they are?

What's your favourite book?
....
....

Villain's name:

What are they like when they are young?

What happens to them?

How do their experiences change them?

How does their past make them the way they are?

Hero's name:

What are they like when they are young?

What happens to them?

How do their experiences change them?

How does their past make them the way they are?

WHOSE STORY?

Your main character might be a person, an animal, an object or a machine. How are you going to tell their tale?

First person

Using the first person makes the story very immediate. Your reader is inside your head and knows what you are thinking.

'I awake shivering and reach out for the warm, soft fur of my mother's pouch. Not there. I stretch my paw further — emptiness. Then I shift and realise nothing is right. The ground is warm, twigs snap under me. Smoke fills my nostrils and I hear the distant crackle of fire.'

This is my baby wombat again. If you write this story in the first person, you will only ever hear the story from her point of view. How much will the wombat understand about wildfires and climate change?

Third person

Writing in the third person gives a sense of distance. You are observing the action. You can tell the story from different characters' points of view.

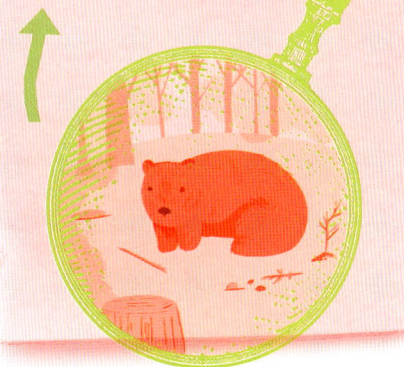

Activity: Write in the first and third person

Ask a parent or carer to help you find a video of Australian wildfires and people who have rescued baby wombats.
- Describe the scene as if you were an orphaned wombat. How might it feel?
- Now tell it as if you were a person involved in the rescue.

Then write a scene from your story in the first and in the third person. See which you prefer.

1. Describe the scene as if you were an orphaned wombat. How might it feel?

2. Now tell it as if you were a person involved in the rescue.

3. Write your story in the first person.

4. Write your story in the third person.

STORY SETTINGS

The setting is the place where your story happens. It can be tiny or huge.

It might be your village or town.

It could be a single tree that is home to animals, as in *The Faraway Tree*.

Your setting can be dramatic – e.g. a remote forest.

If you're writing science fiction or fantasy, your setting might be another planet or a parallel universe.

Activity: Take a movie maker's view
Draw a dramatic action picture. Imagine you've just arrived at the scene.

Activity: Take a movie maker's view cont.

1. Describe the picture you have drawn, like a movie camera taking a wide shot.
2. Zoom in on the action.
3. Now describe the details.

Example

You've just landed on an alien planet. It has a shocking pink sky and two blazing suns. You notice a crater of stinking, bubbling slime. Focus on the inquisitive creatures sliding silently towards you.

Remember

Use all the senses to describe your setting, not just what you see. What can you hear or smell? How does the setting make your characters feel? Scared, curious, delighted?

TIP

If you're looking for good adjectives to describe a setting, try going through the alphabet until you find a word you like.

Example:

You are describing an attic:

airy

bright

chilly

DARK

empty

freezing

Two suns

Stinking, bubbling slime

1. Describe the big picture, like a movie camera taking a wide shot.

2. Zoom in on the action.

3. Now describe the details.

PLOT

The plot is the outline of your story. Every story has a beginning, a middle and an end.

I wrote this story, 'Raised by wolves', based on a true tale.

BEGINNING: set the scene

Six-year-old Rodríguez is sent to work with a shepherd.

MIDDLE: present the problem

The shepherd disappears. The boy survives alone, among wolves.

END: solve the problem

Rodríguez is found when he is 19.

Activity: Draw a story mountain

Add more details to your plot with a story mountain.

1. At the bottom of the mountain, set the scene.
2. Describe your characters and the main problem.
3. Half-way up the mountain, the problems get bigger.
4. At the top of the mountain, there is a crisis.
5. As you come down the mountain, show how the characters will solve the problem. They might fail the first time.
6. At the bottom of the mountain, they solve the problem.

Story mountain example

4. The boy is starving and thirsty.

3. The shepherd disappears, and the boy is left alone.

5. Rodriguez learns to forage for food and catch fish. He sleeps in a wolves' den.

2. Rodriguez is sent away to work with a shepherd. He misses his family greatly.

6. Rodriguez is found. But he never becomes used to human society. He prefers life in the mountains among animals.

1. Rodriguez and his family live in terrible poverty.

'Even if you plan your book, the actual writing is unplanned.' Michelle Paver, author of *Chronicles of Ancient Darkness*

Draw your own story mountain

TIP
'Writing is like a sport — you only get better if you practise.'
Rick Riordan, author of *Percy Jackson and the Olympians* series

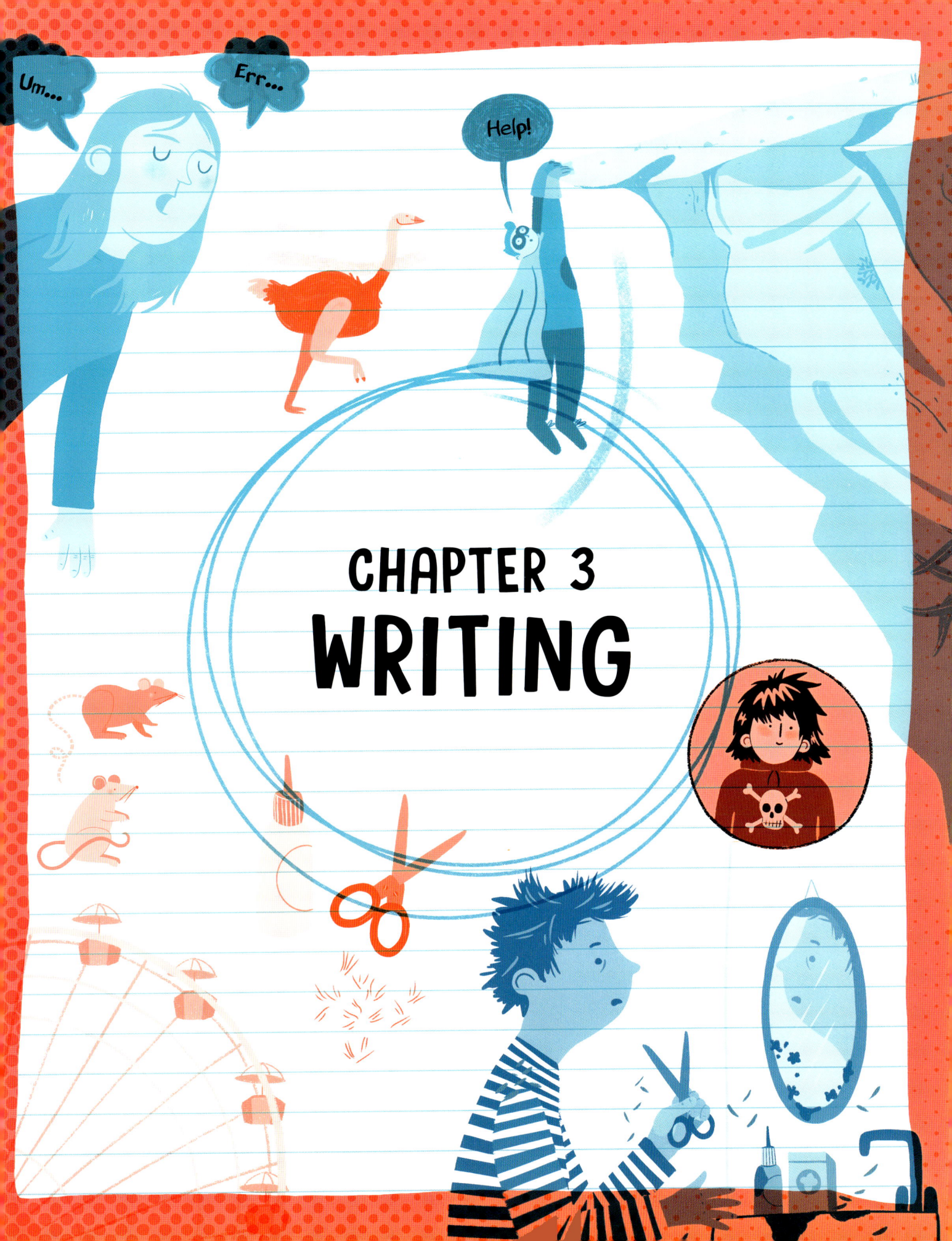

ONCE UPON A TIME

What happens on the first page of the story book you are reading? Are you curious to find out what happens next?

Grab your reader's attention with an excellent opening — either start with the big picture or a detail. Tell or show them something.

Start big and tell

One day in March 2020, every school in the country was shut and every child told to study from home. No one knew when they would return to their classrooms.

Start small and show

Ebony poked her little sister, curled up next to her on the sofa. She was laughing her head off at some stupid cartoon. 'Get off the computer NOW. I've got a lesson. Dad — tell her it's my turn! Dad?'

Activity: Plan the opening of your story

1. What is the setting?

2. Who do you meet?

3. What do you see?

4. Is there some action?

TIP
Introduce an idea that will be important later in the story. Maybe Dad has gone out unexpectedly. He keeps mysteriously disappearing, but you don't find out until later where he's been going.

DESCRIPTION

To write a truly gripping story, describe the scenes so your reader feels like they are right in the middle of the action.

Ace adjectives

Think carefully about the adjectives you use. Whether you are describing the setting, a character or a nail-biting plot twist, bring all the senses into your writing.

Vital verbs

Liven up your writing with a wide variety of verbs. These show what your characters are doing or feeling.

Imagine your character is in danger and needs to alert her friend:

'Quick, hide!' she shouted.

Can you think of some other verbs you could use? e.g.

SCREAMED **YELLED**

SHRIEKED

Adverbs

We use adverbs to describe how we do things, such as loudly or quickly:
Jasmine looked quickly at the galloping monster.

Often you can find a strong verb that works better: e.g. Jasmine...

GLIMPSED peeked

GLANCED

GRRRR....

Activity: Describe places and things

Pick a topic and write a few sentences about it. I've listed some adjectives to help you.

Children in the playground
Sounds: Screaming, rowdy, raucous

School toilets at the end of the day
Smell: Disgusting, foul, stinking

A pet snake
Touch: Scaly, silky, clammy

Your favourite meal
Taste: Delicious, scrumptious, mouth-watering

Woodland walk
What can you see, hear, smell, touch, taste? Scampering creatures, screeching owl, musty leaves, rough bark, tangy blackberries

SHOWING AND TELLING

It's often more engaging for your reader if you show what's happening rather than telling them. Let's say your main character is a girl called Yuki, and she's late for school.

SETTING

Telling

Yuki hated the school. It was an old, ugly, run-down building.

Showing

Yuki sighed. Rain spattered through a broken window as she shoved open the creaky school door.

CHARACTER

You want your readers to know Yuki stands out from the crowd. Compare telling with showing.

Telling

Yuki never wore the correct school uniform and had a wild hairstyle. She was always late for school and sat alone.

Showing

Yuki marched through the classroom towards the empty table, ignoring the stares. She slumped on to a chair, tugging her skull and crossbones hoodie over her spiky hair.

DIALOGUE

You can use dialogue in the same way.

Telling

'Put on your school sweatshirt, Yuki,' Mr Achebe asked.
'No,' she replied.

Showing

'Where's your school sweatshirt Yuki?' barked Mr Achebe.
'I literally have no idea,' she mumbled, gazing at the floor.

Activity: Show not tell
Think of a setting, character and action.

Example:
Setting: children's home
Character: boy with short, fair hair, freckles, tall, shy, brave, clever
Action: new child arrives

What do you want your reader to know about the setting and the character?
How could you show this in their actions?

SPICE IT UP

Your reader really wants to know what your characters look like, feel and experience. You can spice up your writing in all kinds of ways.

Try using similes and metaphors so that your reader will get the picture.

Shaun

Simile

'After dyeing his hair, Shaun decided to give himself a haircut. Three minutes later, he examined his new look in horror. His hair was sticking up around his head **like a toilet brush.**'

Metaphor

'Shaun glanced around the bathroom. Blue dye and shorn curls all over the mirror, the floor, the tiles and every bath towel. **It was a disaster area.**'

Vary your vocabulary

You may find you keep using the same words over and over — 'exciting' adventures, 'interesting' activities or 'delicious' food. Look for different words in a thesaurus.

E.g. 'interesting'

entrancing

FASCINATING   INTRIGUING

GRIPPING   spellbinding   captivating

TIP

When you're reading and find an unusual word or expression, make a note of it to use in a story.

Activity: Improve the word choices

Find some better words to replace the ordinary ones in this paragraph.

It was **raining,** and Shaun was bored. On a whim, he **took a big** pair of scissors and a bag of green hair dye from his brother's shelf. 'They won't think I'm **boring** now,' he thought. He **walked quietly** to the bathroom and locked the door.

Ordinary word: raining

Better words:

Ordinary words: took a big

Better words:

Ordinary word: boring

Better words:

Ordinary words: walked quietly

Better words:

DIALOGUE

How can you make conversations sound natural? A good way to learn is to listen carefully to how people talk. Ask your friends or family if you can record them talking. Play back the conversation and notice how people really speak to each other.

They don't always use full sentences. People use filler words, such as 'like, well, you know'. They hesitate and say 'er, umm'. Sometimes, they interrupt each other.

How people talk

Think about how people talk as well as what they say. They use body language and gestures — shrugging shoulders, smiling, frowning.

Speech tags

Vary your speech tags — the words that show how your character says something. The verb should be a way of speaking, such as shouted, moaned, screamed or whispered.
You can add an action to show how they feel:

'It's happened yet again,' he grumbled wearily.

Or describe their body language:

'Why would you even want a rat?' she asked, shaking her head with a look of utter disgust.

Remember:

When two people are talking, you can often tell who is speaking without speech tags:
'Can you hear that noise, Leila?' whispered Suki.
'No! Inside the spaceship or out?'
'Shhh — it's getting closer.'
Leila hunched further away from the hatch, out of view from the walkway.

Activity: Two people, two opinions

Write a dialogue between a person who has a new pet rat and their friend who hates rats.

PACE

Your story needs ups and downs to keep the action going. It is good to vary the pace, with a mix of fast and slow parts.

Slow pace
- Description
- Long conversations
- Long sentences

Fast pace
- Action
- Short dialogue
- Short sentences

Time

Allow plenty of time to build up to exciting or scary moments in the action — even if they happen in a millisecond. Create tension as the monster hunts down Suki and Leila in their hideout. But in the slower bits, you can speed up — the long night they spend chained up in the monster's lair.

Cliff-hangers

Cliff-hangers are a fantastic way to create suspense.

Example

Set 100 years in the future, David Walliams' *The Beast of Buckingham Palace* has weird and scary goings-on. Several of the chapters end on a cliff-hanger, leaving you wondering what will happen next to the young hero, Alfred.

Activity: Create a cliff-hanger

Write a scene where a small child becomes lost in a crowd.
Use these writing prompts or invent your own.

1. The build-up: exploring the fair — the sights, sounds and smells. The big wheel, dodgems, candy floss. Loud music, laughter.
2. Stopping to gaze at a stall selling enormous lollipops.
3. Suddenly noticing her older sister isn't there any more.
4. Slow down the pace to describe the moment of terror. The feeling of the crowds rushing past, the blaring music, the stench of barbecue smoke — and it's growing dark.

Write here...

'Writing can be a bit like unfolding something... Slowly, the writer reveals what's happening.'
Michael Rosen, poet and children's author

CHAPTER 3: HAPPILY EVER AFTER?

Think about the ending of the last book you read. How did the story finish and did you like it?

Did you know?

Many traditional fairy tales had dark, scary endings, unlike the ones we see in films. In the original Snow White story, Snow White and Prince Charming take their revenge on the queen by making her dance in burning-hot iron shoes until she dies. Nasty!

You can choose from several ways to round off your own story.

Problem solved
The ending might link back to the beginning in some way. Maybe your hero had a problem and now it is solved.

Message
Do you have a message to pass on to your reader? It could be about how people relate to each other or how to solve a tricky world problem.

Ambiguous
You can have an ambiguous ending – it has different possible meanings. Your reader can decide what they think happened.

Twist
Bring in a plot twist at the final moment. Perhaps your hero harbours a dark secret that changes everything...

Cliff-hanger
End on a new problem that your hero will tackle in the next story.

Happy or sad?
It might be a mix – some things work out, others don't.

Activity: Choose the best ending

Write different endings for your story. Test out your ideas on your friends or family and then decide which you like best.

Happy or sad?

Problem solved

Cliff-hanger

Name of my story:

Message

Ambiguous

Twist

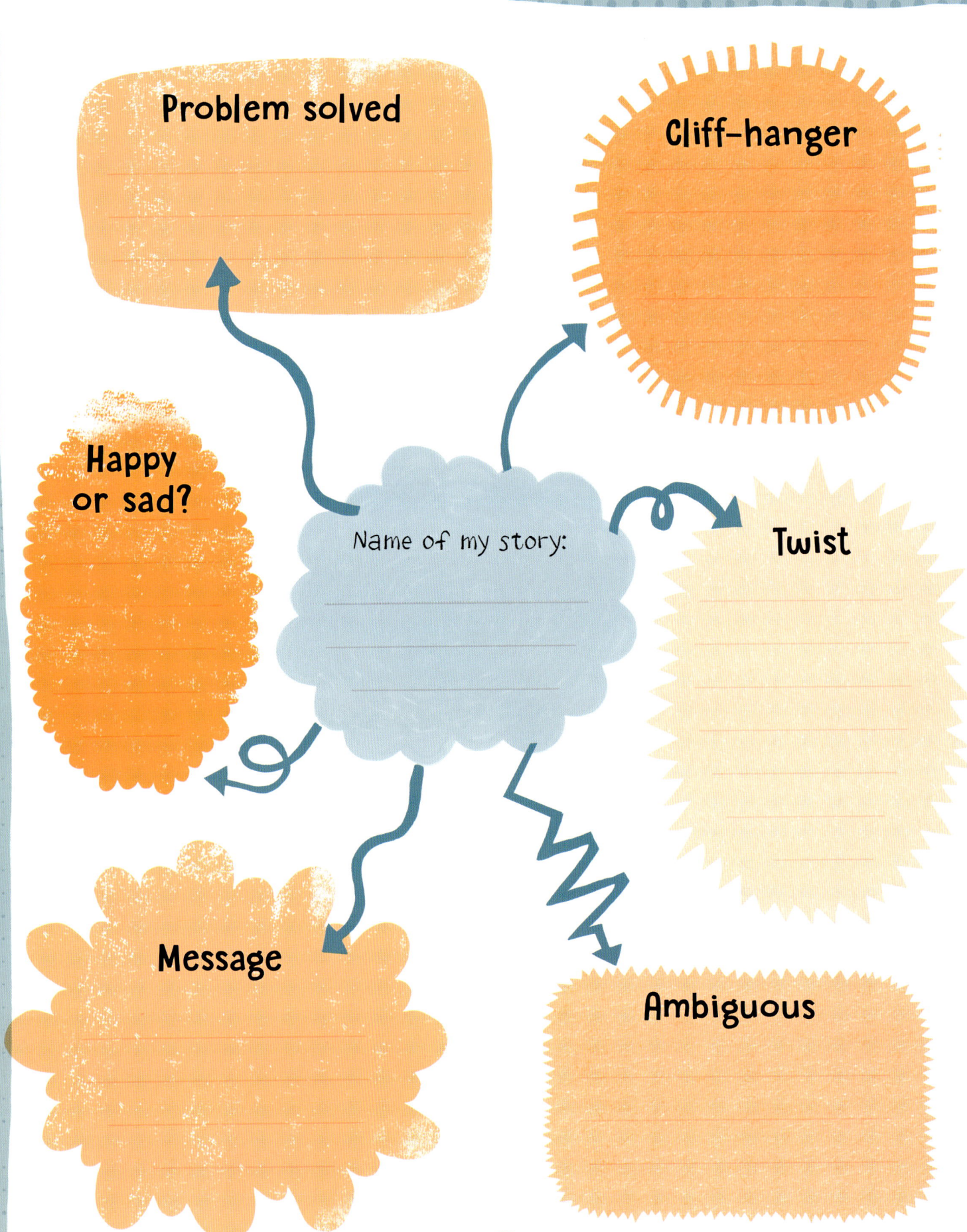

Activity: Choose the best ending

Write different endings for your story. Test out your ideas on your friends or family and then decide which you like best.

Happy or sad?

Problem solved

Cliff-hanger

Name of my story:

Message

Ambiguous

Twist

FAIRY-TALE MASH-UP

Writers sometimes adapt stories they love. How about picking your favourite fairy tale or traditional story and creating your own adventure? Try changing the hero's gender, writing from a different character's viewpoint or setting your story in another place or culture.

Here's my idea for adapting 'Goldilocks and the Three Bears'. The hero is a boy, he has a reason for wandering in the woods, and the people who find him are friendly.

Gideon & the Three Caravans

Gideon has run away from home because he had a big row with his stepdad. He comes across a cosy caravan in the woods, with three tempting meals on the table — spicy noodles, pizza and vegetable curry. Tired after eating his fill, Gideon lies down for a nap. One bed is a cot, another is king-sized, but the third one is just right. When the owners return, Gideon is terrified. Will they be angry and call the police? At first, they are furious but then he explains his story. They help him to call his mum and he works things out with his stepdad.

Activity: Adapt a fairy tale

Fill in the boxes for the traditional tale, then plan your story.

Traditional story:	Your story:
Main character:	Your character:
Setting:	Your setting:
Plot:	Your plot:
Ending:	Your ending:

COMIC STRIP

Plan your story

If you enjoy drawing, you could create a comic-strip story. It's simple to adapt the story mountain:

1. Show the setting and introduce your characters.
2. Describe the problem.
3. The troubles grow bigger.
4. Crisis!
5. How will the characters solve the issue? They might fail the first time.
6. They resolve the problem.

Characters

For a very short story, have just one or two characters. Use your drawings and dialogue to show what they look like, and how they talk and move.

Setting

It's easiest to have just one setting for the action.

Plot

Decide on the problem, how it develops and how your characters will solve it.

Speech

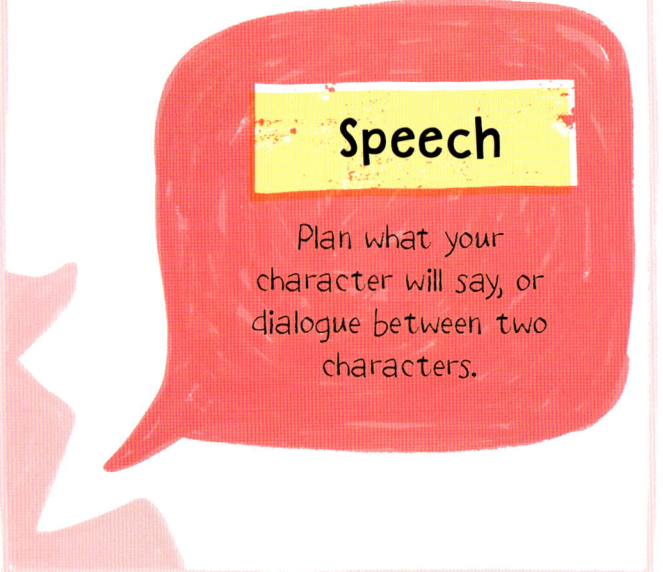

Plan what your character will say, or dialogue between two characters.

Activity: Make a six-box comic strip
Use the story mountain to plan your story.

Example: The pedal bike and the sports car

1. Show the setting and introduce your characters.
A race across a bustling city between a super-confident sports car and a battered racing bike.

2. Describe the problem
Bike thinks it can never beat the speedy sports car. Car zooms off into the lead.

3. The troubles grow bigger
Car hits traffic. Bike slips in between the cars.

4. Crisis!
Car overheats and breaks down.

5. How will the characters solve the issue?
Bike takes the lead and pedals over the finish line to victory.

6. They resolve the problem.
Cyclist goes to help car driver, and they become friends.

Try your own six-box story:

Try your own six-box story:

ANIMATION

If you want to bring your story to life, why not make a stop-motion animation? Create your animation with Lego® characters, modelling clay or toys.

To start

First, watch some short stop-motion animation videos on YouTube for ideas.

What you'll need

- A plain backdrop, such as a wall or board
- Characters
- A phone or tablet with the StopMotion Animation app.

Storyboard

Write your plot. Then make a storyboard – like a comic strip, but with more frames (see opposite).

TIP

Once you are confident with making movies, try adding dialogue.

How to film

Imagine you're making a cops and robbers movie, with a police officer chasing a suspect. Place your characters in the starting position and take a photo. Move the characters a little and take another photo. Repeat until the chase is over, and the officer has caught the suspect — or the suspect has escaped.

Choose music to go with your movie to make it more entertaining.

Activity: Storyboard your animation

Draw a storyboard for a cops and robbers movie, with a frame for every stage of the action.

Draw in the boxes below.

- Who is the robber? What do they steal?

- How do they get away? Running, driving, cycling, flying...

- The police officer gives chase.

- Does the officer catch the robber? Or does the robber get away on their own or with help?

- Ending: handcuffed robber is dragged off to the police station or escaped robber celebrates.

Notes

REAL-LIFE STORIES

Who do you admire? Maybe it's a campaigner, sports person, pop star, vlogger or an actor. Why not write their biography? You could retell an extraordinary event.

Activity: Research your project

Libraries

Books are a great place to start. If you are writing about a historical event, research what life was like at the time. Discover what people ate and wore, their homes, schools and jobs. If it's a biography, explore the place where your character grew up

Websites

Ask an adult to help you to find reliable websites. Start with encyclopaedias, often available through your local library.

Interviews

If you're focusing on a living person, try contacting them to ask for an interview.

Where to begin

When writing about an event, you can describe the build-up then the episode and how it changed the world. Alternatively, begin with the drama of the event, then explain how it all happened.

Biographies

It sounds obvious to write about a person's life from cradle to grave. But starting with a dramatic moment brings your reader straight to the heart of the tale. This is how I started my recent biography of J. K. Rowling:

'On Friday, July 21, 2007, a long line of little witches and wizards were waiting for the clock to strike midnight... Younger ones were napping in sleeping bags while older fans discussed popular Harry Potter characters, played games, and munched snacks. Something magical was about to happen.'

Research your story and make notes here.

SCIENCE FICTION

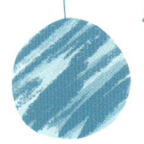

Take your story into space, voyage to other worlds or travel in time to the past or future. The wonderful thing about sci-fi is that you can create your own world. Draw the places, people, creatures, plants and machines. Make a map so you know where everything is when you're describing the action. The reader should be able to view the scene in their mind's eye.

Familiar Features

Make sure you include some familiar features, so that readers can relate to your setting. Even in other solar systems, there might be schools, parents, pets — and annoying little brothers or sisters.

Friend!

Aliens

If you have non-human characters, use the activity in the fantasy section on page 71 to help you develop them.

Time Travel

Imagine what our world will be like in the future. Think about our daily activities — eating, learning, playing, sleeping. How might we do them in 50 or 100 years' time?

FANTASY

Fantasy writing is as varied as your imagination. Your story could be historical or involve magic, myths, legends or heroes. If you're inventing a magical world, you can use the sci-fi tips on pages 68-69.

Legends

Legends are about real or invented people. Many tales are told about them. According to English legend, Robin Hood and his gang of outlaws lived in the Middle Ages. Hiding away in the dense tree cover of Sherwood Forest, they stole from the rich to give to the poor. Historians have uncovered many Robin Hoods, so it's likely that lots of rebels inspired the story. You could take a topic from a legend for your tale.

Robin Hood

Superhero

Superheroes

Do you have a favourite superhero, such as Wonder Woman, Hulk, Spider-Man, Captain America or Black Widow? You could invent your own hero with superpowers.

Myths

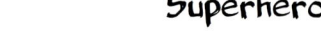
Poseidon

Myths are set in the past, often involving gods and goddesses and extraordinary events. In Ancient Greek myths, Poseidon was the god of the sea. With his three-pointed trident, he made islands rise and shook the world with storms or earthquakes.

Activity: Create non-human characters

Your characters may not be real, but you want them to be fully fleshed-out characters. Describe them in words or pictures. Invent life stories for your main characters (see pages 24-25).

What do they look like?

How do they eat, drink and breathe?

What are their emotions? For example, love, hate, jealousy, greed, kindness.

What are their senses?

Do they have special powers?

WILDLIFE ADVENTURE

An adventure is a fast-moving story. The heroes get themselves into big trouble and struggle to find a way out. But they don't have to be human...

No ants?

I'm so hungry.

Activity: Animal adventure topic

1. Write about your favourite creature, whether it's a tiny, cute hamster or a giant, furry anteater.

_____
_____
_____
_____
_____
_____
_____
_____
_____
_____

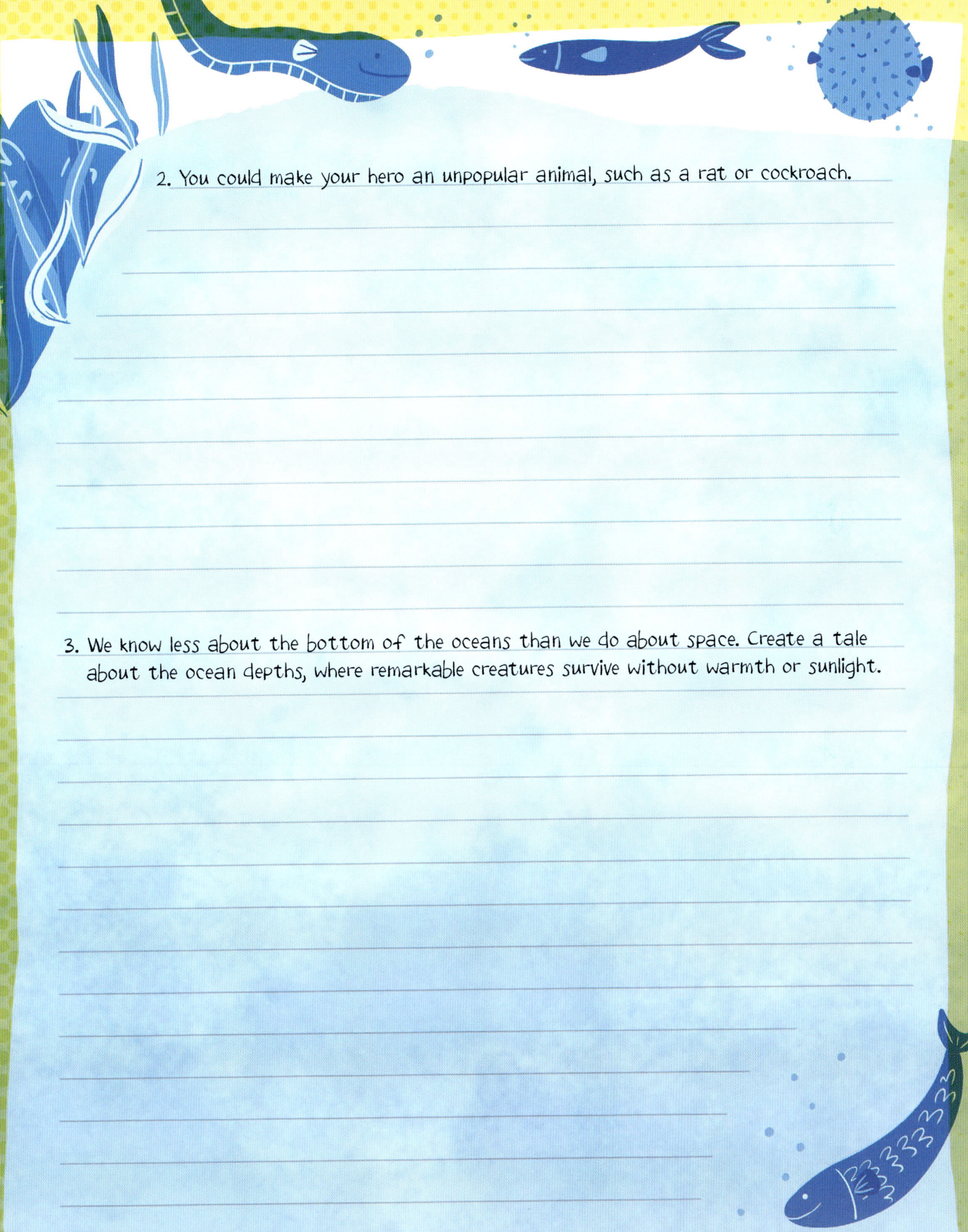

2. You could make your hero an unpopular animal, such as a rat or cockroach.

3. We know less about the bottom of the oceans than we do about space. Create a tale about the ocean depths, where remarkable creatures survive without warmth or sunlight.

Activity: Make a journey stick

1. Find a stick about 30 cm (11.8 inches) long. Attach about 10 elastic bands, or short lengths of wool or string, to fix small objects to the stick.
2. Go for a walk in the park. Look for leaves, acorns or other large seeds, twigs or fallen flowers. Fix them to the stick, starting at the top and working down to the bottom until it is full.
3. Use all of your senses. Record sounds on your phone or write down what you hear: leaves rustling; twigs snapping; birds singing. Note what you smell, too.
4. Afterwards, describe your walk using the objects you found. What do they look and feel like? What did you notice on your journey?

Your walk may spark ideas for a wildlife tale or poem.

Write your ideas here.

WHODUNNIT

Based around a crime, a whodunnit is written from the detective's viewpoint. Your readers try to work out 'who done it', using clues the detective discovers.

Characters

- Create several suspects who all have a motive and could have been at the crime scene.

- The criminal is normally not the obvious person. They appear in the story but may not seem important.

Plot

- Red herrings: The detective goes down the wrong path, following a suspect who turns out to be innocent. This makes your story more believable. In real life, the police often investigate several suspects before finding the guilty person.

- Plot twists: Take your reader by surprise. Maybe there is a baddie among the detectives investigating the crime.

Detective skills

- The crime scene: What clues can your detective spot?

- How do witnesses behave? They might avoid telling the truth to protect someone else.

- Examine people's habits. Did suspects do anything unusual at the time of the crime?

- Evidence: The forensic team examines the scene for DNA.

Activity: Plot a whodunnit

Someone is hacking the school website — breaking into it to cause damage. No one can access the website, and teachers can't email. Who is the attacker, why are they doing it and what do they want? They could be:

- Hackers stealing personal data to sell on the Darknet
- People from a rival school
- A random hacker testing their skills
- A student who had warned the headteacher that the site was not secure

Decide on the motive and plot the story.

CREEPY STORY

Every creepy story focuses on a threat – whether it's from monsters, witches or ghosts.

Create fear

We are frightened of the unknown. It could be a bizarre noise, a weird light in the sky, a strange smell or odd-tasting water. Remember to explore all the senses.

Setting

Your monsters might lurk in stinking cellars, cobwebbed cupboards or airy attics. They may await nightfall to attack and cause mayhem. But an abandoned summer house by the beach at dawn could be just as scary.

Beginning, middle and end

Choose to start your story with a creepy moment or start without a hint of fear. In the middle, build up suspense – your reader only finds out gradually what is going on. What are the monster's powers, and what does it desire?

The climax of the story is the terrifying part, with the showdown between the monster and its victims. In the end, the mystery is revealed. Will it have a happy or a tragic ending? It's up to you...

Activity: Create your creepy character

Draw and describe him, her or it.

6. What does it want?

1. What does it look like?

5. If you can touch it, what does it feel like?

2. What sounds does it make when it's happy / angry / frightened?

4. Does it smell of anything?

3. How does your character move?

FLASH FICTION

These short, short stories are usually between 300 and 500 words long. They can be just 50 words long — or only six!
It is said that the 20th-century US author Ernest Hemingway wrote this famous six-word story:

'For sale: baby shoes, never worn.'

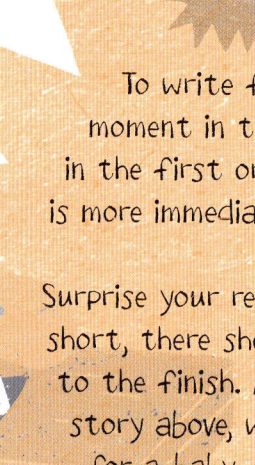

Ernest Hemingway

One moment

To write flash fiction, think of one moment in time. You will have one character, in the first or third person. The first person is more immediate.

Surprise your reader. Even though the story is short, there should be a change from the start to the finish. At the start of the six-word story above, we know that someone had shoes for a baby. At the end, we wonder why the baby shoes were never worn. In a mini story, every word is important. A good title is vital, too.

Activity: Pick a prompt

Use one of these prompts to help you find a flash-fiction topic.
- An important moment in your life
- A strange situation in an ordinary place
- An ordinary situation in a strange place or another world
- Doing something new for the first time
   - Choose an object or an animal and write it from their viewpoint. Only reveal your character at the end.

Have a go at writing flash fiction.

POETRY

A few carefully chosen words in a poem can tell an entire story. To write a poem, you'll need:

Alliteration

Using words starting with the same letter or sound, e.g. 'The crafty cat clambered into the cupboard.'

Words

Either rhyming, using words with similar end sounds such as 'cat' and 'rat' or — not rhyming.

Rhythm

Like the beat in music. You might decide to have 6 beats in each line, e.g. 'The rat sat on the cat'.

Activity: Write an acrostic poem

In an acrostic poem, the first letter of every line spells out a word. This word is the subject of the poem. Your acrostic poem can rhyme, but it doesn't have to. The lines can have a different number of beats.

Buzzes around a beautiful flower.
Enters it to find sweet nectar inside.
Exits with nectar and covered in pollen.

You could write an acrostic poem about a season, festival, plant, animal or friend.

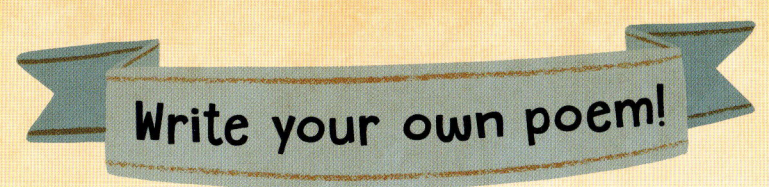

Haikus

A haiku is a traditional Japanese poem. It has 17 syllables in a 5, 7, 5 pattern. Here's an example:

Autumn haiku

Leaves on the wet path
Shrivelled, scrunchy, crackly, brown
Under my big boots.

Write your own haikus here.

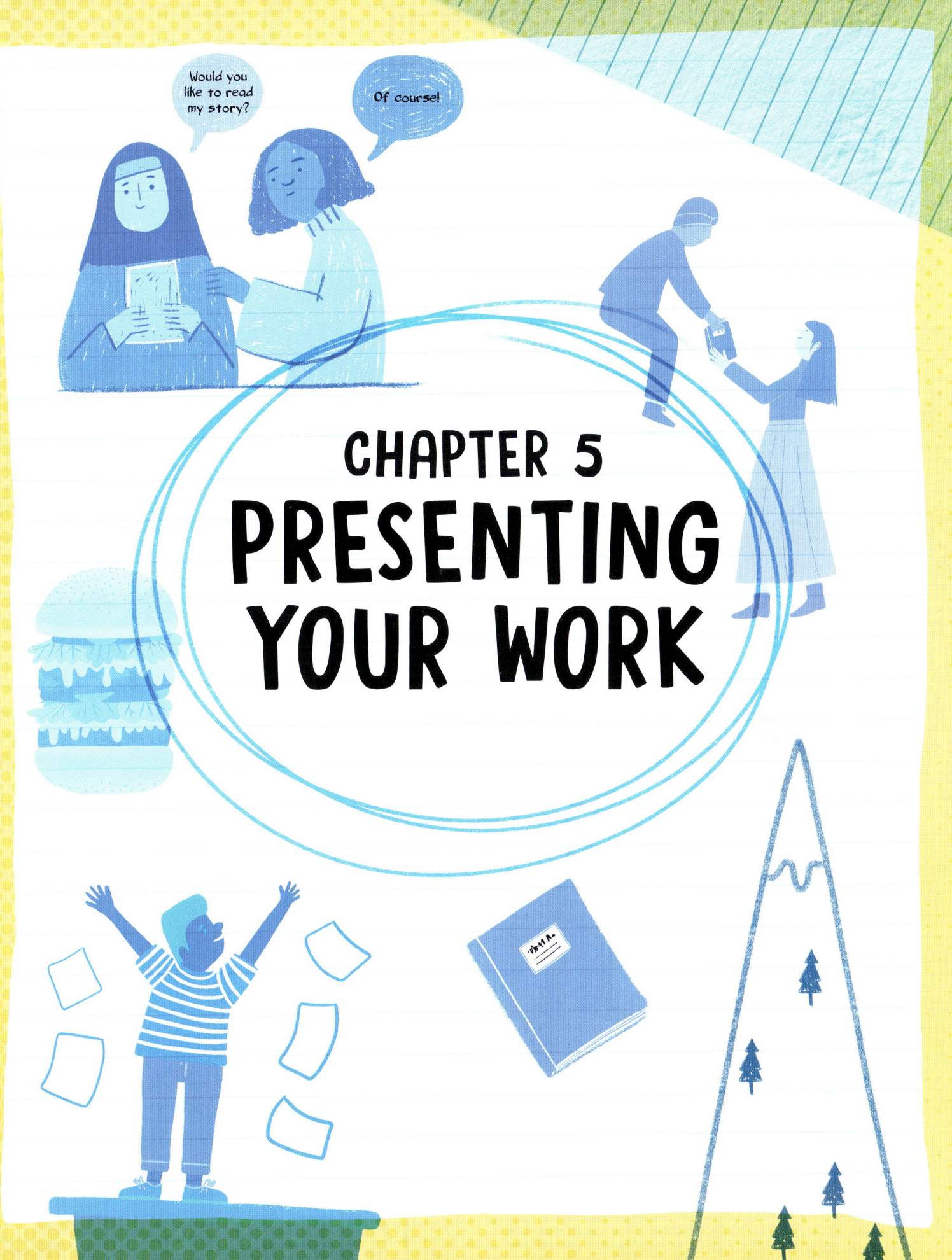

TRY AND TRY AGAIN

Authors never write a perfect draft first time. They rewrite their work again and again and again... until they are happy with it.
The first stage is to check what you have written.

Content

Setting needs more description

Too much description

Cut out bits you don't need. Some parts may have too much description, slowing down the action. Take out any character that doesn't play a useful role.

Is there anything you should add? Maybe a scene needs more detail.

Plot

Does the plot work? Make sure it fits the story mountain.

Beginning and end

See if the opening is exciting and the ending satisfying. Have you tied up the loose ends or are you leaving the ending open for the next story? If there's a twist, check you've provided clues earlier in the story.

TIP
When I'm rewriting, I put the deleted parts in a spare text file in case I change my mind and want to use them.

Activity: Check the plot

1. Look at your story or another short story.
2. Read the first sentence of every paragraph.
3. Can you work out the story line from those sentences alone? If so, you have a clear plot.
4. If not, check the order of your paragraphs. Maybe you need to swap some of them around so that the story works better.

List the first sentences of your story here.

NOTES

Activity: first lines

Here are the first lines of the paragraphs in a traditional story that I rewrote. Can you guess the story? Now fill in the rest of the paragraphs.

A shoemaker had some very bad luck.

In the morning, just as she was about to sit down to work, she saw two shoes standing completely finished on the table.

Soon after, a customer came into the shop.

That night, she cut out the leather and left it on her table.

The following morning, she found the four pairs were made.

Now one evening, not long before Christmas, the shoemaker finished cutting out the leather as usual.

On the stroke of midnight, two little elves came into the room and sat down by the shoemaker's table.

The next morning the husband said: 'Those little people have brought us wealth, and we really should show them how grateful we are.'

The shoemaker said: 'That's a great idea. It's the least we can do after all the elves have done for us.'

At midnight, the little people came bounding in, expecting to get to work at once.

They dressed themselves quickly, putting on the pretty clothes.

They danced, skipped and leapt over chairs and benches in celebration, before dancing out of the door.

MIND YOUR LANGUAGE

Now look at *how* you have written your story.

Sentences
Good writing has a mixture of long and short sentences. Sentences should never be too long though, or your reader might get lost in the middle.

Vocabulary
Mix it up. If you've written the same word a lot, use a thesaurus to change it to other words with a similar meaning.

Dialogue
Do your conversations flow well? The best way to check is to read them out.

Language
And last, but definitely not least: please check your grammar, punctuation and spelling.

Consistency
Check your characters. If you've said in chapter one that Lloyd has hazel eyes, be sure not to refer to his brown eyes in chapter four. Check the settings. If the spaceship hatch is at the front, don't say it's at the back in another chapter.

TIP
Read your story aloud. It will help you to notice mistakes. If you run out of breath reading a sentence, you know it needs some punctuation or you should divide it in two.

Activity: Take the editing test

See if you can spot 10 mistakes in this text. Circle them and write the corrections at the side. The answers are on page 103.

A shoemaker was down on her duck. All she had were the lether for one pair of shoes. that evening, she cut the leather into shape and left her work on the counter to finnish in the morning. She went quietly and calm to bed, hoping for a miracle The next morning, as she hurried to her counta, she was astounded to spot two shiny shoes on the table. They were neatly maid with tiny stitches. A perfect pear.

e.g. This sentence needs a full stop.

FEEDBACK

You become so close to your own story that it's hard to know how to improve it. Ask someone you trust to read it and say what they think. Even better, swap your story with another writer and give each other feedback. Use the checklists on pages 88 and 92 to help guide you.

Top feedback tips

- Read the story and think about it before giving feedback.

- Use the 'feedback sandwich'.

1. Start with a positive comment. What did you like?

2. Make a helpful suggestion to improve.

3. Finish with another positive comment.

- Make precise comments. Instead of saying 'Ruth is boring', you might say, 'I suggest adding more details about Ruth's character.' Check the section on character (pages 22–23) for ideas.

- If there's a part that doesn't work, ask yourself why. Does it fit with the rest of the story? Is there too much description? Could it be left out?

Activity: Write a book review

Practise giving feedback by writing a review of a book you've read recently. First, read other book reviews so you can see how people write them. I structure book reviews like this:

1. Write the book title, author and date it was published.
2. Give a summary of the plot and main characters. Make sure you don't include any spoilers. This can be quite hard to do!
3. Talk about the strengths and weaknesses of the book.
4. Give your overall view of the book. How many stars out of five would you give it?

You could try to publish your review on your school website. Ask an adult to help you post it on a popular book-selling website.

Write your review here:

SHARING YOUR WORK

If you're proud of your story, please share it with friends and family. I hope you'll be inspired to keep writing. Why not join a children's writing group in your local area or online?

Enter a short-story competition

- First, read the winning entries from previous years to see the kinds of stories that the judges enjoyed.

- If the judges provide feedback on your story, read it carefully so you can improve next time.

- If you don't win a prize, just try again!

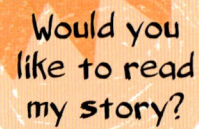

Self-publishing

It's quite easy to submit your story to a children's writing website or create and publish a digital book yourself. Different apps allow you to write the text and upload your own photos or drawings. You can publish your book online or have it printed. Ask friends and family members to review your book to create interest — good reviews sell books. Then ask a parent or carer to help you promote your title on social media.

Your book in print

Would you like to try publishing your story as a printed book? Check the lists of publishers in the latest *Children's Writers' and Artists' Yearbook*. You may find it in your local library. Look carefully for companies that publish just the kind of book you have written. Check what you need to send to discover if they like your story. You never know — you might be lucky!

Activity: Build a goal ladder

Set yourself goals for your creative writing. Think about your end goal — what do you hope to achieve? Find or draw pictures to show it. Put your goal at the top of the ladder.

Use the steps to identify small goals on the way to the top.

Example: Jacob's goal ladder

7. End goal: enter a short story competition.

6. Edit my story.

5. Write my story.

4. Complete the activities in this book.

3. Write for 5 minutes every day.

2. Learn 5 new words every week.

1. Read a book for 10 minutes every day.

Now set your own goals.

- Think about your end goal — what do you hope to achieve?
- Put the goal at the top of the ladder.
- Find or draw pictures to show it.
- Use the steps to identify small goals on the way to the top.

WRITE TO A PUBLISHER

So you want to get your book published! Here's how to write to a publisher. You could send an email, or why not print and post a proper letter? Here's how to write the letter.

Cath Senker
45 Primula Road
Hove
BN3 8AP
Tel: 01273 392871

Submissions Editor
Tansy Press
100 Great Flora Street
London NW1 1BQ

5 December 2022

Dear Editor

I am sending you my graphic novel, *Wombat in a Wildfire*, aimed at 7–9 year olds. Imagine a baby wombat's terror, waking up alone in the charred remains of a forest, with her mother nowhere to be seen. Horrified by the destruction, young wildlife volunteers have launched a rescue mission, and this baby is among the lucky survivors. But will the baby wombat ever be able to return to her forest life?

I've seen that Tansy Press produces graphic novels for primary children to teach them about environmental issues in an engaging way. *Wombat in a Wildfire* would fit well with other titles on your list, such as *Tsunami Survivors* and *Rachel and the Re-wilders*.

I understand that you will reply to me within three months if you are interested in *Wombat in a Wildfire*.

I look forward to hearing from you.

Best wishes,

Cath Senker

Write your own letter

GLOSSARY

Adjective A word that describes a person or thing, such as 'curly hair'.

Adverb A word that adds more information about a verb or an adjective, such as 'gobbling greedily'.

Biography The story of a person's life.

Character Usually, a person or an animal in a story. It could be something that is not alive, like a robot.

Cliff-hanger A situation in a story that is very exciting because you cannot guess what will happen next.

Consistency Keeping how you describe a character or place the same throughout, e.g. where things are in the setting.

Darknet The hidden Internet that you can only access with special software.

Dialogue A conversation in a story.

Draft A rough version of writing.

Edit To improve a draft of writing.

Fantasy A type of story that is set in a world that does not really exist and involves magic.

Feedback Telling someone how good or bad their work is, and giving advice on how to improve it.

First person Writing the story as if one of the characters was telling it, using 'I'.

Freewriting Writing freely for a few minutes to get down your ideas.

Genre Type of story, such as fantasy, science fiction or whodunnit.

Inspiration Finding ideas from things you see, hear, read or experience.

Landscape Everything you can see when you look across a wide area of land.

Legend A story from ancient times about people and events that may or may not be true.

Metaphor A word or phrase that is used to describe somebody or something in a way that is different from its normal, everyday use. A metaphor shows that the two things have the same qualities e.g. 'My nan is a dragon.'

Motive A reason for doing something.

Myth A story from ancient times, especially one that was told to explain natural events or to describe the early history of a people.

Outback The area of Australia that is a long way from the coast and the towns, where few people live.

GLOSSARY

Pace How quickly things happen in a story.

Plot The series of events that form a story.

Science fiction A type of story based on imagined scientific discoveries of the future.

Setting The place where a story happens.

Simile A word or phrase that compares something to something else, using the words 'like' or 'as'. E.g. 'My brother runs like the wind.'

Speech tag The words that explain how somebody says something in a dialogue. E.g. 'Stop right now!' she yelled.

Stereotype A fixed idea or image that many people have of a certain type of person or thing, but which is often not true.

Storyboard A series of drawings or pictures that show the outline of a story.

Suspect A person that the police think may have carried out a crime.

Suspense A feeling of worry or excitement when you think that something is going to happen.

Thesaurus A book or website that lists words which have similar meanings in groups.

Third person A way of writing a story in which the person telling it is not involved in the story.

Twist When there is a sudden turn of events in a plot to surprise the reader and take the plot in a new direction.

Verb A 'doing word', such as eat, play, swim.

Answers to page 93 editing activity

A shoemaker was down on her duck **luck**. All she had were the lether **leather** for one pair of shoes, that **That** evening, she cut the leather into shape and left her work on the counter to finitsh **finish** in the morning. She went quietly and calm **calmly** to bed, hoping for a miracle. The next morning, as she hurried to her counta **counter**, she was astounded to spot two shiny shoes on the table. They were neatly maid **made** with tiny stitches. A perfect pear **pair**.

INDEX

A
acrostic poems 84
alliteration 84
animal stories 72-73

B
biographies 24-25, 65
book reviews 95

C
cliff-hangers 48-49
competitions 96
consistency 92
conversations 46

D
describing
    characters 22-23, 26-27, 71, 81
    places & things 41
    scenes 31-32, 40-41, 68-69
detective stories 76-77

E
editing 88-89, 92-93
endings 52-53

F
first person 28
freewriting 21

G
goal ladders 97

H
haikus 86

I
idea clouds 13

J
journey sticks 74

L
legends 70
letters to publishers 100

M
metaphors 44
mind maps 17
movie maker's view 31-33
myths 70

N
nature 16, 72-74
non-fiction writing 65
note-making 16-17

O
objects 16
openings 38-39

P
prompts for stories 82

R
reading 10-11, 12
research 65

S
self-publishing 96
short stories 82
show or tell 22, 38, 42-43
similes 44
speech tags 46
story boards 62-63
story mountain 34-35, 58-59
superheroes 70

T
third person 28

V
vocabulary 40-41, 44-45